Merch: Zero to Hero

A modern, comprehensive guide to Merch by Amazon

by Antonis Tsagaris

ANTONIS TSAGARIS

Merch: Zero to Hero

Copyright © 2018 Antonis Tsagaris

DEDICATION

I dedicate this book to my wife and son. They are a constant source of inspiration. My son is also a constant source of poop and pee but he's very cute so I forgive him.

CONTENTS

ACKNOWLEDGEMENTS

This book wouldn't have been possible without me writing it. So it's all about me! Me me me me me me me me me me me me me me me me me!

I'm the best. Deal with it.

Introduction

In early 2018 (February, to be exact) I stumbled upon Merch by Amazon. I don't remember how I found out about MBA. Unlike FBA (Fulfilled by Amazon) and KDP (Kindle Direct Publishing) none of my friends had heard about it and there wasn't a lot of buzz online about its possibilities.

At that point, I decided I had to learn everything about it so I started visiting forums, doing Google searches about every single aspect of the program and bought about ten e-books about it on Amazon.

Those books were not what I expected. One of them was seven pages long and was horribly written and formatted. Another one was just a collection of links to YouTube videos. Yet another one was a collection of outdated (as I realized later) blog posts compiled haphazardly into a 'book'. And so on and so forth.

All those books had something in common. Three things, in fact

1. They were the top of the funnel for further promotions by the writers, in the form of services, courses etc.

2. They were the sort of minimum-effort junk that you can crank out in half a day

3. They were horribly outdated. In fact, if you follow the instructions in one of those books closely, your t-shirts will get removed by Amazon before you can say 'account suspension wtf'. Moreover, some of the MBA success stories from 2015 to 2017 sounded not just extremely optimistic but also deluded and downright comical in the Merch By Amazon conditions of 2018.

But forget about all that. What bothered me the most about those books was what cynical cash-grabs they were: do you know the point at which self-appointed gurus start selling you books and courses about that new "amazing opportunity"? **It's when that opportunity is no longer amazing enough for them to continue making bank directly through it.**

Because let's face it: you are not working under the same circumstances that those gurus were working in back in 2015 and they know it. *And you never will*, for the following reasons

1. **Timing**: those guys got into Merch By Amazon at its infancy. Good for them but everybody agrees that at that point you

could've uploaded a t-shirt saying 'I just sharted' or 'Bread' on it and you'd still get a sale.

2. **Saturation:** Similarly, even if you have a good idea for a slogan or a pun, it's quite possible that someone has already thought of it first. I was *really* looking forward to publishing my '2B or not 2B' pencil lover shirt until I found out that there were at least a hundred other shirts already in Amazon with the exact same pun. Bummer.

3. **The inherent disadvantage of being in lower tiers:** I'm not just talking about the fact that you can only post ten shirts to start with. That's a problem that's easily dealt with as I will explain later. No, I'm talking about the fact that when something new happens (eg. the ability to promote your designs, new types of merchandise) you won't have immediate access to it. So Guru Numero Uno gets to saturate the niche before you've ever had the chance to post a single design.

After reading everything I could, watching tons of videos and browsing Reddit communities for hours, I started creating my own shirts and uploading them. That was when I finally realized how MBA really works, what it takes to succeed and that it's not the get-rich-quick scheme some people think it is.

That was also when I realized that there is no actual in-depth, well-written, definitive book about how MBA actually works in the new, more competitive conditions you'll find yourself in in 2018 and beyond. I'm hoping that this book is going to be that definitive tome.

Let's get going!

Why Merch (& maybe why not)

Do you know how many Print-On-Demand (POD) sites exist out there?

Neither do I.

I know of at least 10 off the top of my head but I'm pretty sure there are many, *many* more.

So why should you go to the trouble of designing and uploading those designs on MBA, especially when MBA requires you to submit an application and *maybe* get accepted to the program **vs** any other POD that just lets you sign up and start uploading?

Two words: **organic traffic**. Also, three more words: **intent to buy**.

In the same way that people go to Google to search for information and on Facebook to pretend that they are amazing all day, every day, people go to Amazon to purchase stuff. They have the money and they intend to use it. Plus, everybody knows what Amazon is.

So you have this perfect storm of millions of people wanting to buy something *right now* going to a site that is the de facto mall of the web.

This is simply not the case with any of the other POD platforms. People going on Redbubble or Society6 are probably also primed to buy something but the amount of people visiting those sites is insignificant compared to the traffic that Amazon pulls. Go on, ask your mom or your grandpa if they know what Redbubble is. Then do the same for Amazon. I'll wait.

I'm not saying 'don't post to other platforms'. It would be wrong to rely solely on MBA for your POD strategy and that's the reason I'm including a short chapter on other PODs at the end of this book.

However, please understand that, for all its shortcomings, MBA is your best chance of making sales without having to drive external traffic to your listings. And it's free, with printing, shipping and returns handled by Amazon.

'Shortcomings? You mean this thing has shortcomings?'

Yep. **Lack of product variety** is one of them. Where other PODs allow you to print on shirts, hats, towels, tote bags, phone cases and skirts among many others, on MBA you get two types of shirts, long sleeve shirts, hoodies, sweatshirts and PopSockets.

Another thing you'll have to deal with is the **draconian enforcement (sometimes to a ridiculous degree) of copyrights and trademarks.** Obviously, it's not a good idea to put out Star Wars merchandise on any POD platform but on MBA you may get designs rejected because you used the word 'classy' in your product description and 'classy' is somehow trademarked. True story. More on this in the relevant chapter.

Finally, **the tier system can (and will) drive you mad.** When you start out, you're on Tier 10. That means that you can only have up to ten designs available for sale at any given time. This is very limiting and it can take forever to make your first sale.

Then you have Tier 25 (up to 25 designs for sale), Tier 100, Tier 500, Tier 1000 and so on.

Because getting sales on MBA is largely a numbers game, you'll have to tier up fast. More on tiering up in the next chapter.

Oh, hey - one last bonus shortcoming: **any design you upload will get removed if it doesn't make a sale within 180 days**. You can re-upload it if you think that it has unfulfilled potential but it can get pretty tedious, pretty fast.

Signing up

If you want to request an invitation for MBA (and you should, if you ask me) go to https://merch.amazon.com/landing and fill out the form. Most people will get accepted to the program but you usually have to wait for up to a week to get in. Use that time to prepare some designs!

It has been hypothesized that MBA does not like people in the same household having different accounts, so in case someone that lives with you already has an account, use a VPN service and a different bank account to request an invitation.

If you have a portfolio site where you already showcase your work, include that information in your application too.

Tiering Up Effectively

To start making any real money on MBA, you need to tier up. To tier up, you need to sell shirts.

Thankfully, you don't have to sell ten shirts to get out of Tier 10 these days. Having a single sale and most of your ten slots filled means that you'll get tiered up to Tier 25 soon.

This also goes for Tier 25, Tier 100 and so on. Having about ten sales and most of your slots filled in Tier 25 means that you'll get tiered up to Tier 100 after a while.

I got tiered up to Tier 500 after having most of my 100 slots filled and having made 33 t-shirt sales.

My suggestion is this: **DO NOT wait for an organic sale in Tier 10. Buy one of your own designs** and get out of Tier 10 *fast*.

In fact, I would go as far as to suggest that you buy yourself out of Tier 25 too (like I did). Spend 130 bucks or so and get to Tier 100 quick.

After getting to Tier 100, stop buying your own shirts and start developing a strategy to get some organic sales. More on this in the following chapters.

'But Antonis, I don't live in the US so I can't buy my own shirts! Your plan sucks'.

Listen, pal: your *mom* sucks.

Also, here's a trick to buy your t-shirts internationally:

Simply use a forwarding service like *shipito.com* or *myUS.com*. If you have never used a forwarding service before, it works like this: you create an account and they give you a US address. You use that address as your delivery address and your package goes to their facilities. Then they forward it to you to your actual address, wherever you are.

Yeah, it costs a little extra but it's worth it just to get out of the first couple of tiers.

Rules of MBA

I call them rules, you may call them guidelines. Doesn't matter.

1st Rule: Who am I selling this shirt to?

In general, I'm not writing these rules in order of importance but this one is the exception. **The most important rule of MBA is 'who am I selling this design to?'**

Before you even open your design software to start creating your t-shirt designs you need to decide *who the customer for your design is going to be.*

It is very tempting to start posting abstract, artful designs, especially if you're already a designer, but that's not the way to go on MBA. On MBA you create a focused design to target a niche (or a combination of niches).

For example, your target niche could be cardiologists. In this case, you could make a t-shirt with an ECG graphic and words saying 'World's Okayest Cardiologist'. (I haven't searched Amazon but I'm pretty sure a t-shirt like this already exists. 'World's Okayest *Something*" is one of the most used phrases on MBA shirts)

A combination of niches would be something like "World's Best Cardiologist Mom". This combines the cardiologist niche with the mom niche. The audience for this design will be smaller, obviously, but it also means that there will be fewer designs for you to compete with in the marketplace. MBA is getting pretty saturated these days so combining niches is a way to stand apart.

I understand that this may sound underwhelming, especially if you're a creative person striving for originality but buddy, you're here to make money, not art. And, like it or not, this works (in principle. In practice, you need to do some research these days. More on this later)

Generally, when dealing with niches, there are two ways to go about it.

One way would be to go for **scaled designs**. This means that you create a base design like the aforementioned "World's Okayest..." shirt and change the text and/or the graphic to target a variety of niches. So something like "World's Okayest

Dermatologist/Pediatrician/Dentist/Stonemason/Busboy/French Restaurant Chef/Windsurfer" and so on. This way, you can target a lot of niches with a minimum of effort.

The other way requires you to have **domain expertise or knowledge**, either because *you're part of the niche you're targeting* or because you've done extensive research and learned the terms, vocabulary and colloquialisms of that specific niche.

The second way takes a lot more time and effort but, in my experience, it pays off. Amazon is chock-full of cheesy, scaled, minimum effort designs (some of them are so overused that they have become a joke within the Merch by Amazon community). They may have sold when the platform was younger and less saturated but nowadays there will be tons of "Straight Outta..." and "What's your superpower?" shirts for any niche you can think of.

My suggestion is this: to start with, create t-shirts that people in your profession would wear. Think of puns and in-jokes that they would love to wear on them.

Don't you have hobbies? Create t-shirt designs for your hobby too. Chances are that even if you're a pickled onion jar collector, some people will share your perversion.

If you've just tiered up and need to fill some slots (it's a shame to have them sitting, in my opinion) then crank out some minimum effort designs and start replacing those when you have better, more targeted designs.

2nd Rule: Can I compete or is the niche oversaturated? BSR and number of competitors

Once you've decided on a niche, go ahead and do a search on Amazon. If you plan to create designs for photographers, write something like "photographer tshirt" and prepare to be disappointed. There are currently **901 results** for those keywords. The chances of your design standing out among those 901 other shirts are very low.

Should you give up? Nope. Try to get a bit more specific. Search for "wedding photographer tshirts". Nice! **701 results**. That's better but probably still too many.

OK. Let's try "wedding photographer tshirts for men". Hey! **395 results.** Much better! Want to go deeper? OK, Leonardo diCaprio, let's try "funny wedding photographer tshirts for men". **234 results**, a mere five pages of results! Now your design stands a chance of being discovered among the others, if you use these keywords in your brand name, title and bullet points.

Some people claim that Amazon's search algorithm includes something called a "freshness boost". This means that (if the so-called freshness boost actually exists) recent submissions appear higher in the search results list for a limited amount of time to give them a chance of being seen and bought. Hopefully it's real.

Moving on.

The concept of BSR is something you'll become intimately familiar with as you get more into Merch. BSR stands for **B**est **S**ellers **R**ank and the lower it is, the better for a product. A product with a BSR of 10,000 sells a lot. A product with a BSR of 1,000,000 sells less than the former product. Think of it as the charts for products listed on Amazon. The higher a product is on the charts (and hence, the lower the BSR is) the better selling the product.

The holy grail of MBA success is finding a niche (keywords) for which

1. **there are only a few shirts listed**
2. **those shirts have a low BSR**

This means that there isn't a lot of competition (few shirts) and that there's demand (low BSR means that the ones that exist are selling).

Never forget this.

When you search on Amazon, you can see a product's BSR by scrolling down to Product Description (on desktop). On mobile, scroll down and tap on Features & Details and then scroll down again to see the BSR. Use this information to your advantage and you'll start seeing sales, especially as you tier up and are allowed to upload more designs.

3rd Rule: Evergreen, Seasonal and Trending Designs

OK, not really a rule but mostly a look at the three major types of designs as far as seasonality is concerned.

Evergreens are designs that have a potential to sell at any time of the year, like the aforementioned cardiologist t-shirt design.

Seasonal designs are designs created for a specific period, such as Christmas, Thanksgiving, Halloween and Earth Day designs.

Some evergreen designs can have a slight seasonal element, such as a design saying "I thought about signing up for Muay Thai lessons but I just mixed myself a Mai Tai". A design like this can sell all year round but maybe it'll do better during the summer, when tropical cocktails are consumed more often.

Trending designs are designs that are concerned with a specific, transient, ephemeral event and these are pretty short-lived. In my opinion, these are the worst kind of design you can create, since

1. They have very limited shelf life. For example, let's say that you create a design about Trump being a doucheface for the millionth time. You can be rest assured that a couple of days later he'll be a dickhole for the millionth *and first* time and then your design gets forgotten.

2. You don't want to be wasting your slots on these designs, since they are probably never going to sell again. Which means that you also have to take them down, which sucks because it's extra work but also because you now have to create new designs to fill those slots.

3. Their success is not entirely dependent on your ingenuity and creativity. Sometimes, your design's processing time will be excruciatingly long, which is up to Amazon. Sometimes, Amazon will decide that the word 'water' in your t-shirt's title is trademarked and your design will be under review for five days. And sometimes, even if the design gets reviewed and processed in time, the indexing of the shirt (the process which makes the actual t-shirt searchable and, most importantly, sellable) will take too long. All of these factors, which are almost totally out of your control, may conspire to keep your amazing design off the eyes and hands of buyers until the trend has passed and it's too late to sell a shirt.

Trending designs are not all bad, naturally. *If* your design becomes available in time and *if* you hit a trend, you may sell a ton of shirts. Selling a lot of shirts is very cool, since you get a lot of royalties but also because you get closer to tiering up to the next level.

In my opinion, the best strategy is mostly evergreens with some seasonals. This will get you pretty close to the fabled "passive income" a lot of people covet once you have a library of shirts that sell regularly. If you rely mostly on trends and seasonals, you're going to have to constantly maintain your account to keep your momentum.

Designing for Merch

Designing for MBA is similar to designing for any other platform or purpose.

Of course, designing for garments presents some unique challenges and opportunities. In this chapter, I'll share some tips about this kind of design and I'll also suggest some software you may want to use, from free all the way to definitely-not-free.

How to create an effective MBA design

The one thing you have to keep in mind when designing for MBA is this: **how will this design look on the Amazon search results thumbnail?** Oh, wait - let me make an important addition: how will this design look on the Amazon search results thumbnail **on mobile**?

Your text needs to be readable on tiny-sized thumbnails, which means that it's better to use heavy type (regular, bold or black variants of fonts work great for this while thin and light variants are not appropriate) and graphics that are not too detailed.

What should you put on your shirts?

Let's assume that you have a niche that you'd like to go into with some designs.

There are three kinds of designs you can create:

1. Text-only shirts: as the name suggests, on this type of shirt you put only text (like a slogan, a catchphrase, a pun or a saying of any type)
2. Graphic-only shirts: no text, only a graphic
3. Text and graphic shirts: these are the most common shirts on MBA

In my (and many other people's) experience, **text and graphic shirts sell best**. It makes total sense, of course, because people usually buy shirts that say something about themselves - and it goes without saying that the best way to express something on a garment is a combination of text and graphics. This segues very smoothly into the next part of this chapter.

Create designs about *the wearer*, not about the subject

I mean, yeah, obviously the t-shirts should be *about* something but they should mostly be about how the wearer feels about or correlates to the selected subject.

A great example would be a shirt about bonsais. Lots of people are into bonsais so it makes sense to think that some of them would buy a t-shirt about the subject.

That doesn't mean that it's enough to write "BONSAI" on a t-shirt or stick some clip art of a bonsai on a t-shirt and call it a day.

A much better approach would be to put a graphic of a bonsai on a t-shirt and under the graphic write something like "Bonsai Master". This way the shirt speaks **about the wearer**: they are a bonsai master, it's something that defines them.

Similarly, you shouldn't put an image of line dancing on a shirt and write "Line Dancing" on it. Write something like "Line Dancer Extraordinaire". Make it about the wearer.

One last tip: if you're coming from an artistic, creative background, you may have an aversion to cheesy, overused clichés. Forget about your distaste for them: people buy this type of shirt all the time.

If you can find a niche that hasn't been completely flooded already, make variations of the following. They may sound dumb to you but there's a reason there are so many of them.

- **"I never thought I'd be a [** placeholder attribute **] of a [** child's/spouse's attribute **] but here I am, killing it"**. Example: "I never thought I'd be a mom of an amazing dentist but here I am, killing it"
- **"Straight Outta [** something **]"**, in a "Straight Outta Compton" cover parody layout. Example: "Straight Outta Sugar"
- **"I'm a [** something **]. What's Your Superpower?"**. Example: "I'm a Marine Biologist, What's your Superpower?"
- The ubiquitous **"Eat. Sleep. [** something **]. Repeat"**. Example: "Eat. Sleep. Ice Hockey. Repeat"

Again, keep in mind that most niches are flooded with these types of shirts but if you can find a relatively underserved niche and create these kinds of shirts you can still pull in some sales.

Finding Niches with a foreword about getting rich quick

FInding niches is easy. Finding niches that are profitable and not completely flooded is quite a different thing and this is where research, hard work and experimentation come in.

Gurus may have convinced armies of gullible souls that Merch is a get-rich-quick path to success but nothing could be further from the truth.

It may have been a get-kinda-affluent-relatively-quickly path at some point in the past, when competition was non-existent and dinosaurs were roaming the earth. However, them continuing to act like the conditions haven't changed from when they where starting out is dishonest at best and plain sleazy at worst.

So if you're here for a quick megabuck, just throw this book in the trash and buy my beachside property in Ohio.

Otherwise, understand that even MBA requires you to devote quite a lot of time to it and get to work!

Niche Research, Part 1: Find the Niche

Finding niches is the easy part. Really.

Go into Google and write "profitable niches list". Why do we care if they are profitable? Because it means that a lot of people are into them!

I am not even going to give you links - just go through the search results and make a list of niches that excite you even a little bit or in which you have some domain knowledge or expertise.

Domain knowledge matters because if, for example, you've ever done weightlifting in the past you must have gathered some specialized knowledge and terms that may help you create a smart, witty design.

Afterwards, think about the sort of designs you could create for people in the same (or similar) occupation as yours.

Other people's jobs and hobbies can also be great sources of inspiration. Remember that acne-ridden, kinda-stinky nephew of yours that sits menacingly in the corner every Thanksgiving dinner? Ask him about his hobbies and hope they do not include "small animal decapitation". He may be a stamp collector or an indie platformer fan.

One of my best-selling niches is something that I used to make huge fun of my cousin about when he first started doing it. And then I thought "hey!"

More inspiration! I find a lot of inspiration and learn about niches I would never have known about by listening to podcasts. Podcasts are an easy listen while driving, exercising or running errands, so don't let that time go to waste - continue researching even while you're driving!

One example of a podcast that can give you lots of ideas is Oh No! Ross and Carrie! at http://ohnopodcast.com/. Ross and Carrie investigate spirituality, fringe science and claims of the paranormal through the lens of evidence-based science. They were the reason I learned about reiki, firewalking, nootropics etc. If you're feeling dirty, don't worry: you don't have to believe this stuff to make shirts about them!

More podcasts I listen to that have given me lots of ideas are, in no particular order

- Sawbones, a medical history podcast

- Freakonomics Radio
- The Flophouse
- Adam Ruins Everything

Finally, never stop observing the world around you! Just got some coffee and the barista said something clever about cappuccino? Jot it down in your notepad.

Did you buy some paracetamol at 12am and the pharmacist confessed that she is pissed off about the long hours she's pulling? Jot it down! Your next successful t-shirt could be "Exhausted Pharmacist, Will Sell Drugs for Coffee".

Niche Research, part 2: Test the Niche

After you've found a niche you'd like to work in, you have to start researching the niche to see if it's promising.

These are the steps I usually take, and I suggest you do the same:

1. Go into <u>amazon.com</u> and **search for your niche** (add "shirts", "t-shirts", "tees" or "tshirts" at the end of the search query)
2. **See how many results come up.** If they are over 400, try to make the niche you'll be working in more narrow. You don't want your design to get lost in a sea of hundreds upon hundreds of shirts. If there are over 400 results over tens of pages, how deep do you think a prospective buyer will go?
3. **Narrowing down** works like this: if you've decided to work on the reiki niche and there are too many results when you search for "reiki t-shirts", go back to Google and type something like "types of reiki". A quick search just revealed that there are at least five types of reiki. One of them is called "rainbow reiki". Aww.
4. Armed with that knowledge, search for "rainbow reiki t-shirts". I just did that. "Reiki t-shirts" returns 144 results. "Rainbow reiki t-shirts"? That query returns 18 results! Yes!

5. **Now start clicking on the t-shirt results and scrolling down to see their BSRs** (best sellers rank). Remember that the lower this number is, the more it's selling.

6. If a shirt has no BSR associated with it, it hasn't sold a single one. That happens. **Alarm bells should go off when all or most of the shirts in your niche have no BSR.** No-one is buying them. This niche sucks balls. ABORT!

7. **If enough t-shirts have a BSR** (I would say that even half of them having BSR is enough for you to go into the niche) **then design a shirt in that niche** (more on this later) and upload it (more on this *also* later. It's going to be a long night)

8. Wait. **Wait longer.** If you're on tier 10 or tier 25, consider buying one of them for yourself and hide it in the darkest recesses of your closet. Unless you're into this kind of thing. I know I hid mine. If you have your 10 slots full, in a couple of days you'll be tiered up to T25.

9. At some point, the shirt may sell. It may even sell multiple times. **If you see repeat sales (even if it only sold twice) on a particular shirt in a particular niche, double down on that niche.**

10. **Doubling down on a niche involves creating and uploading more in that particular niche.** In this case, for example, I'd create one shirt for each type of reiki. That's five more shirts that have a chance of selling!

Here's an interesting thought: sometimes you'll find out that the shirts in a particular niche have low BSRs, like #10,000. This means that the shirt is selling like hot cakes. This is amazing and it should make you excited for your own shirts in that niche, especially if the niche is underserved, with only a few bad quality designs.

However, sometimes the BSR will be in the millions, which means that the shirt is selling like once or twice a month. Sucks, right?

OF COURSE IT DOESN'T, DUMMY!

Imagine, if you will, that you have a library of 100 shirts and each one of them is selling twice a month. That's 200 sales. If your average royalty is $5 per shirt, that means that you'll be making around $1000 per month with designs that don't sell that much.

This is why tiering up matters so much. Having a lot of slots to experiment with and create a library of regularly-selling t-shirts (even if they are selling only once or twice a month) is what is ultimately going to make you successful on MBA.

So never underestimate designs or niches with designs that have a high BSR. They can still be very lucrative if they are part of a larger library.

How To Design

Teaching you how to design is way outside the scope of this book.

Graphic design is a huge subject and a book about Merch is not the best place to do it.

However, I can give you some pointers and even a link to a free series on vector graphics design by yours truly.

First, let's discuss the software you can use to design your shirts.

Design Software

Here's a list of paid design software you can use

- **Adobe Illustrator** and/or **Adobe Photoshop**: the priciest option, since it requires a subscription for every piece of software you want to use. I only have a subscription to Illustrator since it's more than enough for creating t-shirt designs. Other people feel more comfortable in Photoshop. The two programs are not interchangeable (Illustrator is great for vector graphics, Photoshop is great for raster graphics and photo manipulation)
- **Affinity Designer** and/or **Affinity Photo**: Affinity's Illustrator-like and Photoshop-like program, respectively. While not as powerful as Adobe's program's *yet*, they are each a one-time purchase of around 50 USD/euros so they end up being much cheaper if you're going to be using them for more than a couple of months. Keep in mind that, while I said that they are not as powerful as Adobe's programs, they are more than capable of creating t-shirts.
- **CorelDraw Graphics Suite**: This includes software for both vector and raster manipulation and design. I have never used CorelDraw's suite so I don't feel qualified to discuss it but it's

being used by pros for graphic design so I guess it should also be good enough for t-shirt design. The suite is pretty expensive too.

Here's a list of free design software you can use:

- **Gravit Designer**: Gravit Designer is a fantastic free vector graphics software program. It's not as powerful as the Illustrators and Affinity Designers of the world but it's still plenty powerful for t-shirt design. It's a free download for Windows, macOS, Linux and (get this) Chrome OS. It also includes Gravit Cloud, which lets you save your work on their servers and load it from wherever you are! Gravit Designer was recently acquired by the Corel corporation (creators of the CorelDraw Graphics Suite I mentioned earlier) so I hope it stays free in the future.
- **GIMP** (GNU Image Manipulation Program): think of the GIMP as a free Photoshop. It's very, very powerful and it even has a modification called GIMPShop that makes it work a lot like Photoshop. Definitely recommended.
- **Inkscape**: Inkscape is the free, super-powerful alternative to Illustrator. If your budget is limited, it's a fantastic vector graphics program that'll let you do pretty much anything you want.

Most important design skills for t-shirt design

If you're an experienced graphic designer, you'll be pretty familiar with what follows. If you have never done graphic design before, these skills should be enough to let you create some beautiful, eye-catching designs

- **Resizing vector artwork**: The web is full of professional-quality vector graphics for you to purchase and include in your t-shirt designs. Knowing how to resize them is pretty vital. Thankfully, it's very intuitive to do in all vector graphics programs. You just click and hold the corner of their bounding box (the rectangle that surrounds them when you import them in your vector graphics program) and drag to enlarge or shrink down. In most programs, holding down Shift or Alt while you drag will keep the graphic proportionate and won't distort it in the x- or y-axis.
- **Drawing text on a path**: this refers to text that seems to follow a shape, like a circle or a stroke. In most vector graphics programs, it's very easy to do: first draw the shape or stroke you want the text to follow and then select the text tool and hover it over the shape. The cursor should change to indicate that you can now click and start typing on the path.

- **A nice library of fonts and willingness to experiment**: as I mentioned earlier, strong fonts with heavy weights are the best fonts to use on t-shirts. These fonts are readable on the search results thumbnails at Amazon. People won't give your design a second look if they can't read what's on the shirt. Later in this book, I'll suggest some fonts that are perfect to use on t-shirts.
- **Creating a distressed look**

As I said, teaching you design is really not the point of this book. However, I also can't stand the thought of leaving you with no guidance.

For that reason, here's a link to a six-part vector graphics series I published on Medium. Don't let the "...for Android Developers" part scare you. It's mostly a couple of lines of code in each part and they are not necessary for understanding the articles. Simply ignore the code.

Vector Illustration Basics for Android Developers at

https://bit.ly/2Mte0mf

Finding Graphics For Your Designs

Let me be clear about something: I have nothing against free clipart and graphics but I would never use them for my designs.

It's mostly a licensing issue: you may find some graphic on a site that claims it's free for commercial use, put it on your t-shirt and then find yourself in trouble for unlicensed use of the graphic (sometimes people upload artwork that requires a license to use on those sites, thinking that they are helping other people).

If that happens, your design will be removed but even worse, after a number of these violations, Amazon may decide to suspend or terminate your MBA account.

There's no reason to take the risk, especially when there are so many vector graphics bundles with a proper license that you can purchase for super-cheap, if you know how.

Here's how.

First, go to the following sites and sign up for their newsletters/offers/whatever. Just give them your damn email and agree to have offers sent to you, whenever they have them.

I should mention that I have no affiliation with these sites and I'm just mentioning them because I'm very satisfied with the quality and quantity of graphics and fonts they include in their regular bundles.

1. **Creative Market** (https://creativemarket.com) : I don't mean to buzz-market here but Creative Market is my go-to whenever I need some graphics, fonts or illustrations. The interface is great, the prices are some of the lowest you can find and their bundles are like treasure chests without the disgusting moss and lichen. They also have some great freebies. Go on, sign up.

2. **MightyDeals** (https://www.mightydeals.com/): Another awesome site with amazing bundle offers. These guys put so much stuff in every bundle that I never have enough time to check everything out. This is why I suggest you keep some rough notes about what is contained in each bundle. Because you may not need that graphic of a mermaid listening to dubstep and farting rainbows *today* but you'll definitely need it someday.

3. **Design Cuts** (https://www.designcuts.com/): If the other two sites I've already mentioned are the approachable hipster designer in slacks, Design Cuts is the gentleman in a fine suit with a stubble beard and a British accent. Exuding class from every pixel, Design Cuts bundles contain stuff you're unlikely to find anywhere else. These bundles are a bit more idiosyncratic and contain some unexpected surprises. Highly recommended.

4. **The Hungry JPEG** (https://thehungryjpeg.com/): I only came upon this site recently. They have some nice freebies, some cool bundles and cheap graphics galore!

5. **Iconscout** (https://iconscout.com/): Iconscout sells icons. However, those icons are (sometimes) surprisingly detailed and can be easily used as graphics on your t-shirts. The best part is that you can buy individual icons for $1 (or slightly more) so it's very easy to find cheap graphics for your ideas. You can also buy icon sets but those are mainly for UI design so you probably won't need them. Unless your t-shirt is *about* UI design, that is.

6. **Free Design Resources** (https://freedesignresources.net/): lots of free stuff on this site but make sure to always read the license! 'Free' doesn't always mean 'free for commercial use'.

After you've signed up for their offers and newsletters, expect to start receiving offers for bundles pretty regularly. The value for money these bundles offer cannot be overstated.

You don't even have to wait: on any of these sites, look for sections called "Current Bundle" or "Current Offers" and they most likely have one (or more) available right now.

By the way, you don't have to only buy bundles. You can also buy individual items at any point. Just search for your niche name and a graphic representing it will likely pop up in the search results, (especially if you're on Creative Market, which seems to have something for every situation).

A tip: always be careful with the freebies on these sites. Their licensing is sometimes limited to personal use, unless you buy them. So always check the license for anything you're using.

A Note On Graphic Formats

When buying graphics, always check the format(s) that you'll receive the graphics in.

These are my two rules. Ignore them at your own peril:

- **DO NOT BUY graphic assets that only contain JPEG files**. JPEG files are horrible for t-shirt design because they don't support transparency. At best, you'll be able to cut them out manually from their background and save them to another format that supports transparency. Not worth the trouble. Next!
- **DO NOT BUY graphic assets that do not state in their description what formats you'll be receiving when you buy**. Because it's totally unprofessional and also, the format may be JPEG. Remember, we hate JPEGs with a passion over here at Merch Towers.

Acceptable formats for t-shirt design work are

- **.ai:** Adobe Illustrator file. This is a vector-based format created in Adobe Illustrator. Affinity Designer can also open these files, although you may have to massage them a bit to use them as intended in that program.

- **.eps**: Embedded PostScript file. Also a vector-based format that can be opened in most graphic design programs, even the free Gravit Designer after a recent update!
- **.svg**: Scalable Vector Graphics file. A vector-based program that's very popular. Again, most (all?) graphic design programs can open this format.
- **.psd**: Photoshop Document file. A raster-based, layered image file created in Photoshop. Less preferable to vector-based files, in my opinion, but still good enough to work with.
- **.png**: Portable Network Graphics file. A raster-based file format originally created for the web. Unlike that goddamn JPEG format, PNG files support transparency, which makes them perfect for t-shirt design, if their resolution is high enough.

Raster vs Vector. What's that all about?

Raster files are bitmaps. Bitmaps are composed of pixels. If you start zooming into a raster-based file (like a .JPEG, fuck JPEGs by the way, or a PNG) eventually it's going to start pixelating, ie. you'll start seeing the individual colored squares it's made up of. It's like seeing a mosaic from far away: from far enough, it looks like a normal picture. Get close enough, though, and you'll start seeing the tiny pieces of rock or glass that make it up.

Vector files are different. A vector-based graphic is essentially composed of curves and lines described by mathematical equations. The advantage is that the graphic is now resolution-independent. You can zoom as much as you want into it or enlarge it to cover the side of a building and it won't lose any of its fidelity. This is why I mentioned earlier that vector-based formats are better for graphic design. You can manipulate them without worrying that they'll degrade.

Finding Fonts For Your Designs

Finding fonts for your designs is as easy (or even easier) as finding graphics for your designs. It's much easier to find free high-quality fonts with permissive licenses, too.

All of the aforementioned sites (Creative Market, Design Cuts, MightyDeals, TheHungryJPEG) carry fonts. However, there are also entire sites devoted to free and commercial fonts. Here are my favorites:

- **The League Of Movable Type** (https://www.theleagueofmoveabletype.com/): A motherlode of free, open-source, super high quality fonts. What more could you ask for? These guys are awesome. Consider buying some of their merchandise if you use their fonts, they deserve it. Particular favorites: **Ostrich Sans, Raleway**, **Orbitron**, **League Mono**.
- **Google Fonts** (https://fonts.google.com/): The Internet Font Central. So many to list. I'm pretty sure that all of the fonts listed on Google Fonts are free for personal and commercial use. However, always check. Also, be warned than fonts that are the result of external queries may not be free for personal

or commercial use. Particular favorites: **Roboto**, **Josefin Sans**, **Lobster**, **Monoton**, **Faster One**, **Bangers**, **Bebas Neue**.

- **MyFonts** (https://www.myfonts.com/home): You won't find many free fonts here (although they offers some weights for free occasionally, so sign up for their newsletter) but the paid ones... oh my. If you have a font budget to spend, this is the place to be. Particular favorites: **Bushcraft**, **Qualion family**, **Vodka family** (probably my favorite display font ever), **Frontage** and **Frontage Condensed**.

- **Atipo Foundry** (http://atipofoundry.com/)**:** Home of the Bariol typeface, The Only Thing I'd Cheat On My Wife With™. You can buy all their fonts with a pay-want-you-want model. Be fair. Particular favorites: **Bariol** (duh), **Cassanets**, **Salome**.

- **RetroSupply Co**. (https://www.retrosupply.co/): Specifically the **Curiosities Font Collection** (https://www.retrosupply.co/collections/vintage-and-retro-fonts/products/the-curiosities-collection). Best $50 you'll ever spend on fonts. Particular favorites: **Palm Canyon Drive**, **Wildfire**, **SOLID70**

Keep in mind that there's usually cross-availability of fonts between these services and if you look hard enough, you can find the same fonts for lower prices. For example, RetroSupply Co have their fonts on

Creative Market too, in addition to their own site. Another example: Frontage (the font) is cheaper on Creative Market than on MyFonts.

A final tip on fonts before I present you with a selection of my favorite fonts for t-shirt projects: fonts on their own are great but matching font pairings are even better. Matching fonts takes a lot of practice and trial-and-error so one way to make this easier is to search Google for (you guessed it) "font pairings". This will bring up a lot of search results with suggested font pairings for beautiful typography. Using more than one font on your shirts (but no more than two) can make the design look more professional and thought-out, if the fonts work together harmonically.

Text Designs, Reloaded

As I mentioned earlier in this book, designs with both text and graphics seem to sell better than text-only and graphic-only designs.

However, there's a third, hybrid category that seems to do great for me: text designs with doodles and other small elements.

Some fonts come with extras. Those extras can vary from cartoony squiggles to full-on clipart elements. The best thing about those extras is that they have been designed with the typeface in mind so you know that they will match the mood and style of the typeface.

So if you're creating a text design and the typeface you're using has some extras, don't hesitate to experiment with them by placing them strategically around your text.

I have purchased a lot of fonts because of their extras. There are some hidden gems out there and I'll mention them below.

Antonis's Favorite Fonts for Garment Design

Here are some of my favorite fonts for garment design. These were selected by me, not only because they look great but also because they are mostly bold, impactful fonts that are easily legible on garment designs, either on small thumbnails or from a distance.

Note: fonts marked with an asterisk contain extras. Fonts marked with two asterisks are free to download.

Dreadful* (https://creativemarket.com/Aiyari/863567-Dreadful-Extras) is an amazing layered font system that's perfect for Halloween or cartoony designs. Very legible even at small sizes, although my recommendation is to make the letters as big as your design will let you. Remember: readability is key.

<u>Fonts in a similar mood</u>: SCURD (https://creativemarket.com/PixelMoshpit/1904506-SCURD), **Horror*** (https://creativemarket.com/prigent/27054-Horror)

Simple Things* (https://creativemarket.com/ianbarnard/1934415-Simple-Things-cute-little-font) is a typewriter-inspired font, perfect for postcards, deep quotes and romantic occasions, eg. weddings.

Once In A Melon*
(https://creativemarket.com/denilchan/2490846-One-in-a-Melon-Font-Doodles%21) is a cute, whimsical font, perfect for childlike, innocent designs.

Fonts in a similar mood: **Highflier***
(https://creativemarket.com/denilchan/1315815-Highflier-Font), **Hello Spring*** (https://creativemarket.com/denilchan/1342049-Hello-Spring-Font), **Childish Reverie***
(https://creativemarket.com/denilchan/1238857-Childish-Reverie-Font)

Jaunt (https://creativemarket.com/ste/8113-Jaunt-8-bit-pixel-font) is a great 8-bit inspired font for retro gaming and 80s designs.

Fonts in a similar mood: **Press Start 2P****
(https://www.dafont.com/press-start-2p.font)

Okashi
(https://creativemarket.com/phitradesign/1571902-Okashi-%E3%82%B7-Typeface) is a Japanese-style font for samurai, ninja and martial art designs.

Montebello
(https://creativemarket.com/ianbarnard/1397992-Montebello-Script-Typeface) is easily my favorite font right now. It comes in two styles, a sans variant that's all caps and looks ***AMAZING*** (capitalized, underlined, bolded and italicized) and a script variant that also looks great. Obviously, they work great together. Highly recommended for summery, travel, nostalgic and art deco inspired designs.

Fonts in a similar mood: Aqua**
(https://www.behance.net/gallery/14884671/AQUA-GROTESQUE-TYPEFACE)

Sugar Boats*
(https://creativemarket.com/VintageTypeCo/1098625-Sugar-Boats-Display-Font) is also retro and reminiscent of Victorian or even Art Deco times. It's highly distinctive and has high legibility and readability. It comes in three variants and they all look great.

Fonts in a similar mood: Frontage
(https://creativemarket.com/juri/2773-Frontage-Complete-Family), **Frontage Condensed** (https://creativemarket.com/juri/2288011-Frontage-Condensed), **Adelios**
(https://creativemarket.com/ilhamherry/2586795-Adelios-Layered-Font-%2850-OFF%29)

Nebula
(https://creativemarket.com/TheArtifexForge/1530770-Nebula-A-Liqui
d-Style-Font) is a sci-fi inspired font, perfect for space- and future-
themed designs.

Fonts in a similar mood: **Hyperion**
(https://creativemarket.com/MehmetRehaTugcu/324418-Hyperion-Typeface
), **Galaktica** (https://thehungryjpeg.com/product/6878-galaktica-font/),
Quantum** (https://www.dafont.com/quantum-4.font)

Bison
(https://creativemarket.com/EllenLuff/2361604-%28NEW%29-Bison-A-
Powerful-Sans-Serif) is a visually strong with hard lines and sharp
corners. It's bold weight is amazing for t-shirt design.

Fonts in a similar mood: Bebas Neue**
(https://www.fonts.com/font/flat-it/bebas-neue)

Vodka
(https://creativemarket.com/Fenotype/2183610-Vodka-Font-Pack-35)
is such an amazing, flexible and readable font. It comes in sans, slab,
pen and brush variants and it's the one I'm using consistently in my
own designs.

Merch Types & Design Dimensions

This is pretty simple: Amazon lets you put your design on t-shirts, long sleeve t-shirts, sweatshirts and hoodies (some people can also put them on PopSockets but we won't bother with those for now).

The design dimensions for everything, with the exception of the front of hoodies are 4500 pixels by 5400 pixels

So in the program you use to create your designs, at the document creation stage (when you select "New…" most of the times) set your design dimensions to **4500px by 5400px** and specify that your design should have a transparent background.

If you *don't* select a transparent background, your design may have a white background, which will print on the shirt, making it look awful (unless you're *going* for awful, in which case do your thing)

As I've mentioned, the only exception to these dimensions is the design that goes to the front of hoodies. In that case, the design dimensions should be 4500px by 4050px.

Don't worry, though: MBA won't even let you upload a design with the wrong dimensions.

Once you have your blank document, fill it with your masterful design, following the rules that I've already outlined in this chapter and export it to PNG.

Awesome! Let's get to uploading. Time to sell some shirts!

Uploading

Is your first shirt ready? Great! In this chapter, I'm going to guide you through the uploading process. I'm also going to give you some pointers about keyword usage and the review process.

Once you've exported your design to the correct dimensions, in your Merch dashboard go to the **Create** tab. Let's go through the screens together.

Screen 1 (Upload Art)

Click the 'Upload' button and select your design from your hard disk or wherever it is you're keeping it. The design is going to start uploading.

On the left side of the page you'll see a drop-down menu that says 'Choose product type'. While you're waiting for the upload to finish, select the product type you want to have your design printed on. For the time being, **ignore everything but 'Standard T-Shirt' and 'Premium T-Shirts'**. These are the garment types that sell well on MBA. Later, once you have a lot of slots to fill, you may want to upload designs on other product types. But for now, focus on standard and premium t-shirts.

Below, you'll see a selection panel that allows you to select what you'll print on the front of the shirt and what you'll print on the back. Each side allows you to select a different design. I generally don't do double-sided t-shirts. It's double the effort and it's more expensive to print so you get less royalties. Also, you don't need to complicate matters right now.

Selecting between a standard t-shirt and a premium t-shirt is something that's totally up to you. The upside of selecting a standard t-shirt is that you'll get more royalties from your sale in comparison to a premium t-shirt, if you sell both at the same price.

For example, say that you're selling a **standard** t-shirt at $19,99 (the standard, preset price on MBA). When you make a sale, you'll collect **$5,38** in royalties. If you're selling a premium t-shirt at **$19,99**, when you make a sale you'll collect **$3,88** in royalties.

So sell a standard one at $19,99 and get $5,38 or a premium one at the same price and get $3,88. Sounds like a no-brainer, right?

And it is.

To start with, only upload your designs on standard t-shirts. When you tier up and have more slots to fill, you can start uploading the same design on both a standard and a premium t-shirt and price the premium one a little higher than the standard one (pricing a premium one at $21,99 means that you get a $5,39 royalty per sale).

We are done with the first screen. Click 'Save Selection to Continue' and let's move on to the second one.

Screen 2 (Build Product)

The first thing you do on this screen is select a fit type. You can choose between Men, Women and Youth.

Unless you have a design that's totally inappropriate for any of those audiences, simply select all three. An example of a woman-oriented design is something that says 'Proud Wife of a Sicilian Firefighter'. In this case, only select 'Women'.

Next comes the really important part of this page: color selection.

You can select up to five colors for every design you upload. Some people mindlessly select five that (they think) even slightly complement their design. But not you: you know better because you bought this book. So here are some pointers:

1. **Only select a color if your design is legible and looks *really* good on it.** Passably legible and kinda-sorta-ok does not cut it at this point. The reason is this: when you submit your design for sale, the Gods of Amazon are going to select a random color (from the five you've selected) and this is what is going to show up in the search results. This means that if you've selected two colors that really complement your design, two

colors that are sort of ok and one that sucks, there's a chance that your design is going to show up in the search results represented by the sucky color. This, in turn, may put off prospective buyers from buying your shirt. And all because you just had to select five colors. Good job, dude.

2. At some point, Amazon let slip that the order in which the colors are placed in the color picker is not random. **They are placed in order of popularity**: shirts with the first color in the color picker sell the most, shirts with the second color sell less than shirts with the first color, shirts with the third color sell less than shirts with the second color and so on and so forth. Keep this in mind when you're selecting colors. I personally hate heather colors on shirts but I almost always select them (unless they look bad, see above) since they are all on the first row.

3. Always remember that you can create variations of your design. If you have create a design that looks good on light colors but you know that dark colors sell better, just tweak the design to look good on darker colors. Then, if you have the slots, publish both. If you don't, publish the one with the popular colors and keep the other one for when you have more slots to work with.

The last part of this page is pricing.

Pricing is a subject of constant discussion in Merch communities.

Some people say that you should price low (eg. $13.99) and increase the price as (if) the shirt starts selling.

Other people say that your minimum price should be $19.99 while other Merchers have elaborate pricing strategies that they refuse to reveal because they consider them to be a competitive advantage.

My take on it is influenced by the current conditions on MBA: almost every single seller on MBA that has been with the program for some time agrees that **designs submitted after January 2018 tend to not sell.** It's a constant mantra on communities: "My 2018 designs just won't sell, no matter how many I upload"

While that's obviously an exaggeration of the situation (I only have 2018 designs uploaded and I sell shirts just fine), it's obvious that 2018 designs are at a disadvantage.

My take-away from the situation? **Do not price low**, unless the design is a minimum-effort text-only design you created in two minutes.

Let me explain: It's pretty obvious (but not conclusive) that the problem with the 2018 designs is (lack of) visibility, either because the visibility is algorithmically limited or because the market is oversaturated, or both. Buyers don't see the shirts, buyers don't buy the shirts and, as a result, sales are low.

In my opinion, since our shirts don't get seen as much, you should try to maximize profit from each sale. I don't think that price makes as big of a difference as people think: the $5 difference in price between a $14.99 tee and a $19.99 tee is probably the price of a double espresso at Starbucks these days. If someone wants your design, they will click the "Buy" button - period.

However, if you created something in a couple of minutes, go ahead and price it between $14.99 to $18.99. You'll still be making some decent royalties and it'll give you the chance to experiment with pricing and find the sweet spot yourself.

Screen 3 (Add Details)

See those 'Brand name', 'Title of product' and 'Key product features (optional)' fields? **These will make or break your product.**

A crap design with good keywords will probably sell.
A great design with bad keywords? In all likelihood, it won't.

First, let me get something out of the way: the field called 'Description (optional)?'. You can neglect filling that if you want - even though most people say that you should write something in it, since it helps Google index your shirt.

I personally never fill it because, according to people in the know, its contents are not treated as keywords on Amazon. If you *want* to fill it in anyway, a good strategy is to copy both 'Key product features' contents into the 'Description' field.

And with that out of the way, let's get down to business!

General Keywording Strategy and Information

To start with, find keywords that are relevant to your niche and design. It's easier than it sounds: if you have even a passing interest in the niche, you should already be familiar with some of its terms, slang and colloquialisms.

If you are not familiar with the niche you're trying to design for, then there are two schools of thought:

- Then why the hell are you even trying to design for it? As you know, domain knowledge is a huge advantage to have when you enter a niche. Go make designs about something you're familiar with.
- No problem. Open Wikipedia, study for a bit, make a quick summary of what you've learned and start designing.

I mostly agree with the first school of thought. A quick skimming of some Wikipedia articles cannot compare with the deep knowledge of a subject you've accrued over years and years of experience.

However, whatever you decide to do, be sure to go to thesaurus.com and find synonyms for the keywords that come to your mind off the top of your head. Your mission, should you choose to accept it, is to imagine what a person looking for a shirt like yours would search for. Synonyms are a great way to boost your design's visibility because one person may search for 'funny cat shirts' while another may search for 'funny kitty shirts'. It helps to have both 'cat' and 'kitty' as keywords in your brand name, title and bullet points. I would personally even include stuff such as 'kitten', 'feline' etc. I would stay away from 'pussy', though, for reasons explained later in this book.

One word of caution relating to synonyms etc: **Amazon does not like keyword stuffing.** This refers to the practice of placing a large number of relevant keywords into your brand name, title and bullet point fields with no regard to syntax, grammar and proper sentence construction in general. For example, don't call your brand "Funny Cat Kitten Kitty Feline Pussy Shirts". Go ahead and call it "Funny Cat Shirts for Kitten and Pussy Lovers". It doesn't make a lot more sense (you just said cat three times) but at least it reads better. Even just using commas between keywords can help.

Brand name

This is where you go general but not *too* general. Be sure to include some high-quality keywords in here, even if it they appear to be too broad: if your t-shirt is about ninjas, a cool brand name would be 'Ninja and Ninjutsu Funny Shirts'

Now, with about a zillion t-shirts about ninjas on Amazon, you wouldn't expect this brand name to boost your search results visibility and you'd be correct - it probably won't by a lot. But it's still better than writing a nonsensical, unrelated brand name like 'Sashamarara' or some shit.

There are people that are doing this because of some misguided notion that they will be able to promote their own clothing brand on Amazon. That won't happen. **Do not try to create an apparel brand on Amazon unless you actively enjoy failing.**

Why? First of all, you're selling on someone else's turf. They make the rules (relating to content, apparel types etc) and you follow. Secondly, marketing using AMS (Amazon Marketing Services) ads is a hassle for MBA shirts and in a constant state of diarrhea-like fluidity. Yes, the situation is just that shitty. At the time of writing, for example, the 'old' AMS is not available anymore and the 'new' AMS is only available to a select few.

But most importantly, your brand name is prime real estate for placing keywords. Do not waste it by trying to become the next FUBU on Amazon.

To recap, use the 'Brand name' field to enter some general keywords relating to the niche you're targeting. If you did your research right, the niches you'll be targeting won't be very saturated anyway so even the brand name can be kind of specific.

Before we move on to the title part of this section, I'd like to mention a couple of things that I like to refer to as the 'Merch Keywording Legends'. This is information that is generally considered accepted wisdom by the community but which I haven't corroborated experimentally (yes, I'm a science man), so take it with a grain of salt.

Merch Keywording Legends

Legend 1: Placing your keywords at the start of your Brand name or Title fields will make your shirt rank better in search results compared to if you placed them later in the field

This suggests that if you intended to name your brand 'Funny T-Shirts for Broccoli Lovers', it'd be better to revise it to 'Broccoli Lovers Funny T-Shirts' which will bring the main keyword ('broccoli") closer to the start of the sentence/brand name field. Same strategy goes for your design's Title field.

Legend 2: The Brand Name and Title fields are the most important places to place your keywords, followed by the bullet points. The Description has no bearing on indexing or ranking the design on Amazon.

If this is true, that means that you should use your limited space wisely and select the keywords that go in there very carefully. Both the Brand Name field and the Title field have a (definitely not generous) limit on the number of characters you can enter. Bullet points allow for more characters but, if this legend is true, the keywords that go in there are considered less important by the algorithm.

Legend 3: Sprinkle the words 'shirt', 'tshirt', 't-shirt', and 'tee', as well as their plural forms all around the brand name, title and bullet point fields.

The theory being that these are the words users add to their search queries when searching for t-shirts and that including them increases your visibility in search. For example, someone will search for 'funny dentist shirts', not simply 'funny dentist'. Obviously, replace 'shirt' etc with the type of product you're putting the design on.

Legend 4: If you stand in front of the mirror and say 'Jeff Bezos' backwards three times during a full moon, your Merch account will be suspended.

Nah, just messing with you.

So, should you believe and follow these legends? I believe so. I mean, why not? They can't hurt and, if true, they'll only help.

Title

You've put some high-quality keywords in the brand name field. Now it's time to add the rest of your very valuable keywords in the title field.

Your title should be descriptive of the shirt: if it has some text on it, include the text in the title. However, always try to save space for the rest of your important keywords. I sometimes do not include to full text on the shirt simply to add some more keywords in the title.

Not much more to add here. Let's move on to the bullet points, AKA 'Product Features'

Bullet Points

Bullet points give you the chance to keyword your listing more liberally, since you have more characters to work with.

For my bullet points, I use a basic template I have developed over months of trial and error which seems to work pretty well. A listing never leaves my mad t-shirt scientist lab without containing the following:

- The perfect gift tee for … (insert target audience here)
- Amazing present for Christmas, Halloween … (insert any other holiday here)
- For men, women, children
- For… (insert family members here)
- Include when applicable: funny, hilarious, witty, vintage, distressed, beautiful, lovely, retro, stylish, snarky, sarcastic, political, text, graphic

An example of completing the brand name, title and product feature fields

Let's say you have a political shirt that says 'Make Racism Wrong Again' (hundreds of these shirts exist on MBA already but I'm using it as an example)

Let's start with the **brand name**. You want something related to the subject matter but it doesn't have to be too targeted. I would go with something like

"**Anti-Racism, Anti-Racist T-Shirts**' or maybe '**Racism and Racists SUCK Shirts**' or even '**Decency against Racism, Racists Tees**'

Notice what I did there: I targeted both 'racism' and 'racist'. I also placed those keywords close to the start of the brand name. Now, whenever someone searches for either of these terms, you'll be in the results. Well, *somewhere* in the results.

OK, let's keep going. Next comes the **title.** First order of business? Include the t-shirt text in the title. So we start with

'Make Racism Wrong Again'

There's still place for keywords on the title. Do not waste it. Start thinking: what are people that are opposed to racism also into? I would append something like 'social justice and equality' so it becomes

'Make Racism Wrong Again social justice and equality'

Perfect. But we're forgetting something, right? What are we selling? Probably a t-shirt. So we just add the word 'tee' to the end of the title and our title is done!
The full title is now **'Make Racism Wrong Again social justice and equality tee'** which is very targeted and also includes the 'tee' keyword in there.

A hint: I always place the word 'tee' instead of 'tshirt', 't-shirt' or 'shirt' in the title because it's the smallest word describing a t-shirt. This leaves more space for more juicy keywords in the title. I place the rest of those in the bullet points.

Another hint: whenever you're submitting a t-shirt design, always check that you didn't write 'shit' or 't-shit' by mistake (even if your design is shitty). Amazon is going to reject your design and you'll get a content policy violation warning.

And now for the product features/bullet points. Let's start by going to thesaurus.com and doing a synonym search for 'racism' and... holy moly: we've struck keyword gold. Here are some nice synonyms:

biased, intolerant, prejudiced, xenophobic

You also get some words related to 'racist'

bigot, fascist, chauvinist, sexist, supremacist, nazi

Wow. Tell us how you really feel, thesaurus.com. Anyway.

Now let's start using the template phrases I've mentioned earlier in this chapter to construct our bullet points

'The perfect gift t-shirt for any man, woman and child that stands against racism, fascism, bigotry and chauvinism. An empowering, political shirt against the rise of nazis in the US. Get it for your activist son, daughter, mom, dad, aunt or uncle'

'This text design will make an amazing present for your loved ones that stand against prejudice and intolerant, xenophobic people. A distressed tshirt, perfect for protests and political rallies. Get it for Christmas, Halloween, Hanukkah or any other holiday'

This looks pretty good! Notice that I've used

- The template sentences I mentioned earlier
- All the variations of the word 'shirt' I didn't use in the title
- Synonyms and terms related to racism unearthed in thesaurus.com
- Family members you may want to get this for
- Holidays during which you can buy this as a gift for someone

Now, this is not an exact science and you'll get better with practice. But try to follow the guidelines I've given you and you'll be off to a very good start!

'What about the description field?' I hear you say. To which I can only answer 'What about it? Just copy and paste the damn bullet points in it'

Tools or How Unoriginality Killed The Improvecat

Do not be fooled. There's a curse upon the land of Merchia, a scourge so evil and insidious that it threatens to bring down the entire kingdom and plunge us into an age of darkness the likes of which we haven't witnessed in a thousand generations.

The curse has a name: it's called 'Improvecatting'.

And if you fall under its spell, you are doomed to wander the Desolation Eternal, an eldritch land where t-shirts are never sold and souls are exchanged as currency among its ghostly inhabitants.

Damn. I knew I should have written that fantasy epic novel of mine before I started writing this book.

But seriously.

Shortly after Merch by Amazon started accepting designers, a tool came out that was bound to change the way Merch by Amazon was used forever.

Enter Merch Informer

That tool is called Merch Informer (https://merchinformer.com) and even I have a subscription to it.

Honestly, it's not a bad tool. Quite the opposite, in fact: it's amazing for keyword research and looking at the competition before plunging headfirst into a niche.

Lately its creators have been adding great functionality like an in-app design program that you can use to create your shirts without leaving Merch Informer as well as informational videos etc.

However, Merch Informer also gave rise to the improvecat, a portmanteau of two words: "improve" + "copycat"

People started using its BSR aggregating function, which let them see the top-selling designs for their selected keywords. This was a recipe for disaster because after people started seeing the top-selling designs for their keywords, they started 'improving' the existing designs by cranking out their own variations of best-selling designs.

As you can imagine, this led to the market for a specific keyword combination/niche to become more diluted than the rum in a tropical cruise ship cocktail.

This has led to today's landscape, in which any moderately successful design will soon be drowned in a sea of all-too-similar designs.

Taking it one step further, you'd better wish that your design is not too successful. If it sells a couple of shirts a month, it stands a chance of flying under the radar and keep selling for you month after month.
If, however, you create a design that's very successful, you can expect the vultures to descend upon you in a matter of hours, eyes gleaming with the promise of profit and fingers eagerly on their mouse, with Illustrator open on their PCs before you can say 'WTF'.

'Boy, you must really hate Merch Informer!'

No, I do not. Merch Informer is a nice tool to have at your disposal. It's not free (it currently costs $19.99 per month) so it's up to you to decide if its keyword research capabilities are worth it to you.

I just hate its abuse, which has led to so much oversaturation in most niches that people are reporting making half the royalties with six times the number of uploaded designs.

Listen to me: improvecatting is no longer a viable strategy. Even if you're the first to 'improve' a successful design, you can be sure that you'll be followed by a hundred other copycats in a matter of hours.

That is why my strategy, and the one I suggest you also follow, is *a lot shirts that sell in small quantities.* Obviously, you can't control the popularity of your designs (one might take off and sell hundreds - in which case enjoy the royalties while they last) but going into micro-niches will almost certainly lead to the strategy I suggest.

More Tools

I'll briefly mention a couple of other tools I use.

The first is **PrettyMerch**
(https://chrome.google.com/webstore/detail/prettymerch-for-merch-by/ahclfnpmodphlaiidnpjlkndabpnihea?hl=en), a Chrome extension that
displays your Merch stats in a beautiful way and also makes a
'cha-ching' (or other) sound whenever you make a sale. PrettyMerch is
free but there's also a paid version which adds some more stats and
extra functionality. I definitely recommend this to everyone, especially
the free version. It costs you nothing and it looks cool.

I also subscribe to the **Merch Momentum**
(https://gumroad.com/l/mIuN) weekly guide, which is sent to
subscribers every Sunday/Monday and contains info about hot new (or
old) niches. Honestly, I thought I needed it at first, until I realized that

- You can find niches literally everywhere. Just develop your
  observation skills and keep a notebook or note-taking app
  handy
- I've never made a single sale from the suggested niches,
  although, to be fair, that might have been my fault.

- You don't know how many people subscribe to the same guide. If a thousand other people subscribe to it, you can imagine what will happen in the suggested niches after a couple of days: they will be flooded with so many designs you won't be able to stand out. In my opinion, **people that create these guides should also let prospective subscribers know the total number of subscribers**. Only then will you be able to make an informed decision about subscribing or not.

A great free resource is the Reddit community **r/MerchPrintOnDemand** (https://www.reddit.com/r/MerchPrintOnDemand/). Visit it for some lively discussion and to meet other Merchers!

DISCLAIMER: I'm not affiliated with any of the aforementioned services. Shame on you for thinking i am.

The MBA Content Policy: How to avoid rejections, account suspension, account termination and venereal disease

MBA is a stickler for detail when it comes to its content policy. The smallest detail can have your design rejected and, after enough rejections or removals because of content policy violations, your account could get suspended or, even worse, terminated.

I do not intend to go through the Content Policy line by line because Amazon has a nice page with a video and everything that explains the situation at https://merch.amazon.com/resource/201858630. I will give you some hints, tips and pointers, though.

First of all, you need to understand that **you cannot, under no circumstances, use copyrighted or trademarked material** for your designs, brand name, title, bullet points or description. If you create a design that's a parody of the classic Coca-Cola script typeface and then use 'Coca-Cola' as a keyword, you can expect that design to be rejected for trademark violation. Here's the definition of a trademark

a symbol, word, or words legally registered or established by
use as representing a company or product.

Thanks, Google.

Similarly, if you create a design that includes the cover of The Beatles'
"Sgt. Pepper" album and upload that to Amazon, it will be rejected for
copyright violation, unless you have the rights to use said cover.

Here's the definition of copyright

the exclusive and assignable legal right, given to the originator
for a fixed number of years, to print, publish, perform, film, or
record literary, artistic, or musical material.

Right now you may be thinking "oh, that's easy! Simply don't use stuff I
haven't created or names of brands and stuff". Essentially, yes. But
also, no.

Amazon is the seller of record when one of our designs gets sold
through MBA. This means that they take no chances, as far as
copyright and trademark are concerned, because they don't want to
get into legal trouble for our designs.

So while you may be thinking "Oh, ok, I won't mention Kim Kardashian, Apple, Dr. Dre, Fanta and I won't include Metallica lyrics on my designs", in reality things are a bit more complicated.

One example is the infamous "classy" case. People were using the word "classy" to describe their designs left and right until some douchenozzle decided to trademark that exact word. Afterwards, people started having their designs rejected because they used "classy" in their brand name, title, bullet points and/or description.

The exact same thing happened with the word "deplorables".

If you're wondering how to protect yourself with all this insanity going on, the truth is that you're never 100% safe. However, you can go to the **United States Patents and Trademark Office** website at https://www.uspto.gov/ (more like webshite, amirite?) and do a trademark search for the words you want to use by going to the "search trademark database" section.

As for copyright, never use material you haven't created yourself, haven't properly licensed (eg. by buying the material from Creative Marker or TheHungryJPEG) or doesn't have a license that allows commercial use (an example of a license that allows commercial usage is CC0 or Creative Commons Zero license)

Please remember that Amazon is pretty draconian about enforcing these rules AND DO NOT TAKE ANY CHANCES. As they say in the Merch community, **if you have to think about uploading a design, do not upload the design.**

As for the rest of the content policy, things are much clearer there. These are the things that Amazon considers objectionable content:

- Pornographic content
- Child exploitation
- Profanity. Fuck!
- Promotion of hate or intolerance
- Human tragedy
- Promotion of violence
- Nazi promotion
- Mental illness (UK specific)

Regarding design & descriptions

- You cannot post a blank design
- Inaccurate product descriptions (eg. your title is "dog playing with ball" and your shirt displays a cat playing with a triangle)

- Requests for positive reviews in the title, bullet points or description of the design
- External contact info (eg. do not give out your email, phone number etc. in the brand name, title, bullet points or description)
- Bad design quality, eg. low-resolution designs

Also, never claim that you'll be donating proceeds from your sales to charity or political campaigns.

Finally, make no claims about speed of shipment or product quality.

As for avoiding venereal disease, always practice safe sex.

Staying motivated

You may not think that you need a pep talk right now, but you will. Oh, *you will*.

Any modern Mercher will go through the six MBA stages of excitement and grief.

1. Excitement stage: I was accepted! Yay! Time to start uploading designs. I should sell at least a couple on my first week, right?
2. Grief stage: It's been five weeks. Why haven't I sold anything? Do my designs suck? Am I an impostor? Is everyone better than me? And are you going to eat that?
3. Excitement stage: Hey, after listening to Antonis, I bought one of my shirts, tiered up to T25 and I just had my first organic sale. Sales should start rolling in now, right?
4. Grief stage: it's been a week since the high of my first sale and I haven't made a second one. The dopamin is wearing off. Maybe I should listen to Antonis, buy another 7 or so of my own designs and get to T100.
5. Excitement stage: Tier 100! I've filled my slots! Time to sit back and enjoy the passive income! I've been selling at least one shirt/day, this is amazing.

6. Grief stage: What am I doing wrong? I have tiered up to T500, filled my slots; why are my sales not 5x my T100 sales? Is this what I got myself into, an endless cycle of joy and self-resentment?

MBA can be maddening. You will want to stop. You will think 'I'm never going to make a sale'. You may even give up for a while. However, here's some wisdom to keep you motivated.

It will take a while

Even if you follow my advice and buy yourself out of the first two tiers, it will probably take a while for you to make a sale. It took me *two months* to make my first organic sale although it first took me a month to realize that I should buy myself out of T10 and T25.

This is normal. Do not get disappointed.

Set realistic goals

 Don't think "I want to make $100 on my first month on MBA". Think more along the lines of "$10 sounds achievable for my first month". And then keep upgrading those goals but stay grounded.

Treat it like a business

Some of you may scoff at my suggestion to buy ten of your own shirts to get out of the first two tiers but think about it: if you lower your price to $13, you will be able to buy ten of your t-shirts for $130. Do you know of any retail business that has a start-up cost of $130?

Moreover, buying your own shirts gives them a nice little BSR boost which means that their visibility in search results will improve.

Finally, you know what most businesses have in common? It takes a while to make some profit. Deal with it.

There will be slumps

Just like any other e-commerce business, MBA is subject to seasonal fluctuations in sales.

Q4 is said to be the best quarter for sales because of holiday gifts etc. This is why we add all those "gift" and "present" keywords in our listings.

Summer sucks. People are out having fun and are not really interested in buying t-shirts. This is from my experience but also from the experience of tens of others in online communities I visit.

You can expect a more predictable experience during the rest of the year.

Don't let these seasonal cycles get you down. Keep your eyes on the prize.

You will most probably not get rich from MBA...

...but it can be a nice source of passive income after a while. If you're making something like $500/month after a year, that's pretty cool.

Consider other online opportunities to supplement your MBA income: people seem to be selling lots of journals on CreateSpace, for example. Throw some of your designs on journal covers and start making sales there too *with the exact same designs*.

Other PODs

"Don't put all your eggs in one basket". That's what grandma used to say.

Actually, she didn't because she couldn't speak English.

But *I* do and I'd like to make a Merch-specific amendment to that saying:

Don't put all your eggs in one basket, unless the rest of your baskets have holes at the bottom

Because, let's face it. Nothing compares to Amazon's organic traffic.

I have uploaded my designs on Society6, Teespring, Redbubble, you mention it.

I've made a few sales (cheap stickers, mainly) on Redbubble. Redbubble seems to be the only real alternative to Merch, not because it has even close to comparable traffic but because you sometimes get organic sales out of nowhere. It's the one other POD that usually gets discussed alongside MBA on forums, FB groups and podcasts and for good reason.

So upload your designs on Redbubble too - it can't hurt. Just keep in mind that people tend to buy artier stuff on Redbubble: abstract geometry, patterns, cute hipster art, line illustrations etc. Your 'World's Okayest Proctologist' design probably won't sell on RB. Also, always enable stickers! Stickers sell on Redbubble.

In fact, if you have the time and inclination, upload them on every other POD service out there but prioritize MBA and Redbubble.

Here's a list of other POD platforms that you can upload your designs to

- Society6 **https://society6.com/**
- Teespring **https://teespring.com/**
- Zazzle **https://www.zazzle.com/**
- Sunfrog **https://www.sunfrog.com/**
- Etsy with Printful integration **https://www.etsy.com/**
- Threadless **https://www.threadless.com/**
- Cafepress, if you're an old man **https://www.cafepress.com/**
- Design by Humans **https://www.designbyhumans.com/**
- Teepublic **https://www.teepublic.com/**
- Gearbubble **https://www.gearbubble.com/**

...and many more, if you want to search for 'print on demand platforms".

Keep in mind that some of these platforms offer a huge variety of products you can place your designs on. You are not limited to a small selection of garments like MBA so if you want to promote an existing brand that people already know about, they are great platforms for that.

Epilogue

Hey, you've reached the end of the book! Thank you for reading this far.

Before you go, I want to remind you of something: if you want to succeed on Merch by Amazon, you have to be methodical about it.

Some people sign up with the impression that they are going to start seeing sales right after they put up their first shirt. So they start refreshing the Dashboard page every five minutes, waiting for the sales to start rolling in.

You know how I know? Because I was one of those people. It's have no qualms about admitting it, I just didn't know any better.

This is the reason I ended up writing this book. You don't have to make the same mistakes I did. You now have a plan. Follow the plan and stick with it and MBA is bound to generate some income for you. However remember that it's not going to be the five or six figures gurus are promising it will be - at least not for a while.

Here's a very condensed summary of what you have to remember:

1. Buy yourself out of tier 10 and tier 25. If you have your slots filled, it will take you about ten sales to get to tier 100 (at least that's the case right now, I'll update the book if this changes).

2. Use my advice to find some niches and sub-niches to get into. Do NOT design for no one. Think of what a customer would wear. It has to be about a subject and especially about their relationship to that subject.

3. Once you find niches that work, make more/similar designs in those niches. They are almost guaranteed to sell.

4. Fill your slots fast - even if it is with crap to start with. Then slowly start replacing the crap with nice designs. It's a numbers game.

5. Use some my tips to create designs that are appropriate for clothing. Big, bold, readable fonts. Nice but not too complicated graphics. Keep the contrast between the design and the garment color to a maximum. Do not select colors (not even a single one) that do not complement the design.

6. Do not put your account at risk with intellectual property theft or trademark infringement. Be careful and purchase a license for the assets you use. There are many cheap options out there.

Finally, remember that the plan is to create a library of designs with each selling about two shirts per month. This will protect you from copycats (people aren't in a rush to copy a shirt that sells twice a month).

Obviously, you can't know how many t-shirts you'll sell. Maybe one of your designs will go viral and sell 40 shirts in a day (which is awesome, enjoy it while it lasts because soon the vultures will descend) but if you're targeting sub-niches, that's unlikely to happen.

To end up with a library of 100 shirts that sell twice a month, you may need to upload 4000 designs. That's OK, no one said that MBA is easy money. As I've already mentioned, you need to put a lot of effort into it.

So log into your account and start uploading! If you need some extra guidance, don't hesitate to contact me at sebastian212000@gmail.com!

merch.amazon.com
request invitation
Sign-in

K.O.

(editor)
pixlar.com
4500 x 5400
→ x 4050   px.
(or photoshop

Create new
Transparent background

pixabay.com
Download image
open image as a layer
free transform
hold shift & enlarge

Trademark search.
TMHunt.com
USPTO.gov

Made in the USA
Columbia, SC
12 November 2019

83099698R00064